Rapunzel

A TRADITIONAL STORY FROM EUROPE

Once upon a time,
there lived a man and his wife
who longed for a child.

The wife often sat
looking out a high window
of their house.
In the walled garden next door,
she could see many fine fruits
and vegetables growing.
But alas!
The beautiful garden
belonged to a wicked witch.

One day, the wife noticed
some crisp radishes
growing in the witch's garden.
"Oh," she sighed, "if only I could have
some of those radishes for a salad."

She craved the radishes so much
that she would no longer eat the food
that her husband gave her.
As time went by, she grew weak and pale.

Her husband became very worried
and begged her to tell him what was wrong.
"I have a craving for radishes," she replied.
"If I cannot have some, I will die."

Although her husband
was very much afraid of the witch,
he loved his wife and would do anything to please her.
So, in the shadows of evening,
he climbed over the wall and picked some radishes.

He hurried home with them to his wife
and chopped them up for her into a crisp salad.
"Delicious!" she exclaimed.
"I feel so much better already."

But a few days later,
she again began to crave radishes.
"Cost what it may," her good husband sighed,
"I must get my wife what she desires."

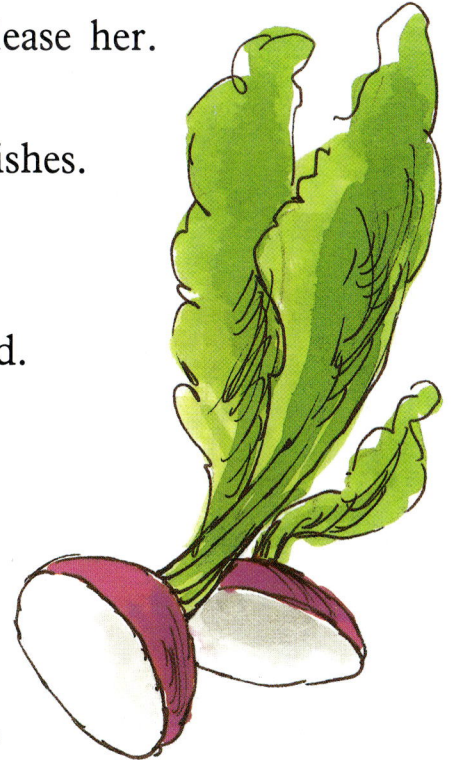

Once again, he waited until evening
before climbing over the wall
and into the witch's garden.
But just as he began to pick the radishes,
the witch appeared.

"How dare you enter my garden!" she cried.
"You have stolen my radishes
and must be punished."

"Do not put a spell on me!"
pleaded the poor man.
"My wife said she would die
if I did not pick her some."

"Very well," she replied.
"You may pick all the radishes
your wife desires.
But when she has a child,
you must give it to me."

The terrified husband agreed
and hurried home with the radishes
for his wife.

In time, a child was born
to the man and his wife.
The witch named her Rapunzel
and took her away.
She grew into a beautiful girl
with long, golden hair.

When Rapunzel was twelve years old,
the witch locked her up in a tower
in the forest.
It had only one small window,
from which she could not escape.
Whenever the witch wished to visit her,
she stood under the window and called:

>*Rapunzel! Rapunzel!*
>*Let down your hair.*

On hearing the witch's voice,
Rapunzel would let her golden tresses
hang out the window
for the witch to climb up
into the tower room.

One day, a young prince
came riding through the forest
and found the tower.
As he stood beneath it,
he heard a beautiful song.
It was Rapunzel, who often sang
to pass away the time in her lonely prison.

For many hours, the prince searched
for a way into the tower.
Finding none, he rode back home,
but he could not forget the sweet voice
he had heard.
He returned again and again
to listen to it.

One day, as he stood behind a tree,
the prince saw an ugly old woman
come to the foot of the tower.
He heard her call out:

> *Rapunzel! Rapunzel!*
> *Let down your hair.*

A plait of golden hair
tumbled down the side of the tower.
The old woman climbed up the hair
and disappeared through the window.

That night, the prince stood
beneath the tower and called:

>*Rapunzel! Rapunzel!*
>*Let down your hair.*

Once again,
out tumbled the golden tresses,
and the prince climbed up the hair
and through the window.

At first, Rapunzel was very much afraid,
as she had not seen a stranger before.
But the prince was gentle and kind
and told her how he had been
so enchanted by her song
that he had to find her.

Rapunzel was so beautiful,
the prince fell in love with her
and begged her to go with him
and be his wife.

"I would come gladly,"
Rapunzel replied,
"but how can I escape from this tower?"

Together they made a plan.
Each time the prince came to visit,
he would bring a skein of silk.
Rapunzel would secretly spin it
into a ladder.
When it was long enough,
she would climb down the ladder
and escape with the prince,
back to his palace.

At first, all went well with their plan.
As the witch visited during the day,
the prince came at night,
so she did not know of his visits.
The ladder grew longer and longer,
and Rapunzel kept it safely hidden
in a corner of her room.

But one day, she made a mistake.
When the witch came to visit her,
Rapunzel said without thinking,
"How come it takes you so long
to climb my hair,
when the prince comes up here
so quickly?"

When she heard this,
the witch was furious.
"You wicked girl!" she screamed.
"I locked you up from the world,
but now I hear you have had a visitor.
You have deceived me
and must be punished!"

With that, the jealous witch
grabbed a pair of sharp scissors.
Snip! Snip!
She cut off Rapunzel's beautiful hair,
which fell in a heap of gold on the floor.
Then she took Rapunzel
to a forest wilderness many miles away
and left her to die.

But even then, the witch's revenge
was not complete.
Returning to the tower,
she tied Rapunzel's hair
to a hook on the windowsill.

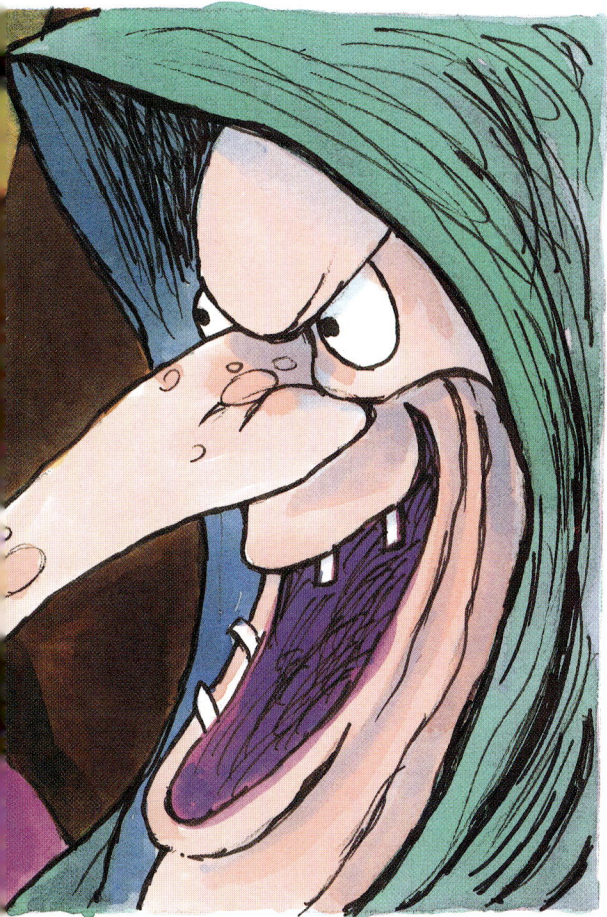

That night,
the prince visited the tower
once again.
Not knowing what had happened,
he called as usual:

> *Rapunzel! Rapunzel!*
> *Let down your hair.*

The witch let down the long hair,
and the unsuspecting prince
climbed up into the tower room.
To his horror,
instead of being greeted
by the beautiful Rapunzel,
he came face to face with the witch.

"I will punish you
for visiting Rapunzel!" she cried.
"I have sent her away to die.
Your eyes will never see her again!"

In terror,
the prince leapt out the window
and tumbled to the ground.
Although he was not killed,
he fell into a thorn bush
and was blinded.

For many days and nights,
he wandered helplessly through the forest,
weeping at the loss of his bride.
By chance, he finally came to the wilderness,
where Rapunzel had managed to survive
on wild fruits and berries.
He heard her voice and called out to her.

When Rapunzel
saw her beloved prince,
she took him in her arms and wept.
Two of her tears fell on his eyes.
The witch's spell was broken,
and he could see again.
They were both overjoyed
to find one another.

Rapunzel and the prince
returned to his kingdom,
where they lived
a long and happy life together.
And as for the witch,
she was never heard of again.